Canada

Authors	Linda Milliken
	Kathy Rogers
Illustrator	Barb Lorseyedi

Reproducible for classroom use only.
Not for use by an entire school or school system.

EP077 © GHC Specialty Brands, LLC, 1997, 2002, 2007
401 S. Wright Road
Janesville, WI 53547

Table of Contents

The Hands-on Heritage series has been designed to help you bring culture to life in your classroom! Look for the "For the Teacher" headings to find information to help you prepare for activities. Simply block out these sections when reproducing pages for student use.

Canada

With a land area of almost 10 million square kilometers (3,860,000 square miles), Canada is the second-largest nation in the world. However, much of the land is in or near the arctic region, making it almost uninhabitable. There are also large areas of undeveloped wilderness. The vast central prairies are rich in farmland. The remaining land is rich in natural resources—fish, furs, timber, and minerals. The landscape is covered with numerous lakes and waterways.

Canada is made up of 11 provinces—Alberta, British Columbia, Manitoba, New Brunswick, Newfoundland, Nova Scotia, Nunavut, Ontario, Prince Edward Island, Quebec, and Saskatchewan—and two territories, the Yukon and Northwest Territories. Each area has its own distinctive characteristics and economy.

Project

Make a map of Canada indicating each province/territory and the capital of each.

Materials

- blank map of Canada
- colored pencils
- atlas or map of Canada

Directions

1. Color each province and territory a different color on your Canada map. Label each one.
2. Use the atlas to identify the capital cities of each province/territory and add them to the map, marking each with a star.
3. Add geographical details like major rivers, bodies of water, and mountain ranges.

For the Teacher

Make a copy of the map of Canada on page 4 for each student.

Canada

EP077 Canada © GHC Specialty Brands, LLC

Canadian Flag

In 1964, Prime Minister Lester Pearson proposed a new Canadian flag. At that time, Canada used the Red Ensign, which included the British Union Jack, as its national flag. A parliamentary committee recommended a flag with an 11-point maple leaf on a white background, with a broad vertical red stripe at each end.

Because the proposed flag contained no reminders of Canada's ties with Great Britain, some Canadians felt it was designed to reduce French resentment toward the English. The Canadian Parliament debated the flag issue for 33 days. Parliament adopted the new flag in December, and it became Canada's official flag on February 15, 1965.

Project

Make a collection box that features a Canadian flag on the lid.

For the Teacher

Copy one Maple Leaf Pattern (page 7) per student.

Materials

- red and white construction paper
- Maple Leaf Pattern
- shoebox
- scissors
- pencil

Directions

1. Cover a shoebox and its lid with white construction paper.

2. Trace a maple leaf onto red construction paper. Cut out the leaf and glue it to the center of the lid.

3. Cut two wide strips of red construction paper. Glue one on each side of the maple leaf.

4. Begin a collection of postcards, newspaper articles, and other memorabilia that focus on Canada. Take time to share the contents of your Canada box as the school year progresses.

Maple Leaf

The sugar maple tree grows across Canada from Newfoundland to Manitoba. It can be found as far south as the Great Lakes. Sugar maples may reach a height of 41 meters (135 ft). The trunk of a mature tree may be 1.5 meters (5 ft) across. The sugar maple has gray bark and dark-green leaves. In autumn, the leaves turn to yellow, orange, and red.

Canadian settlers built their homes using lumber made from the hard wood of the maple tree. During the 1700s and 1800s, maple sugar ranked as an important food item; it was less expensive than imported sugar cane. People traded it for various foods and services. The importance of the maple tree to the growth of Canada was recognized in 1860, when the maple leaf was made the official emblem of Canada.

Project

Make a step-by-step guide to making maple syrup, and create a Maple Leaf Mobile.

Maple Syrup Guide

Directions

1. How do you get maple syrup from a maple tree? Starting with the following Web site: http://www.ontariomaple.com, do research to find out the process.

2. After you've gathered your information, write or draw a step-by-step guide to maple syruping.

For the Teacher

1. Have students examine some maple tree products. Put maple syrup and sugar-based syrup out for the students to taste-test. Can they distinguish between them? Do they prefer one over the other?

2. Find a sample of maple wood or ask your local lumber yard for a sample. Compare it to a sample of pine. Can students tell why maple is designated as a hardwood?

Maple Leaf Mobile

Materials

- wire hanger
- scissors
- Canadian travel brochures and magazines
- yarn
- starch
- hole punch
- paintbrush
- red construction paper

Directions

1. Use the Maple Leaf Pattern to outline and cut three to five leaves out of colorful pictures of Canada. Also cut out three to five leaves from red construction paper.
2. Paste each picture leaf to the back of a construction paper leaf and punch a hole in the top of each.
3. Write a fact about Canada on the red side of each leaf.
4. Cut yarn into various lengths and tie one end through the leaves and the others around the hanger at various lengths.
5. Hang the mobile from the ceiling.

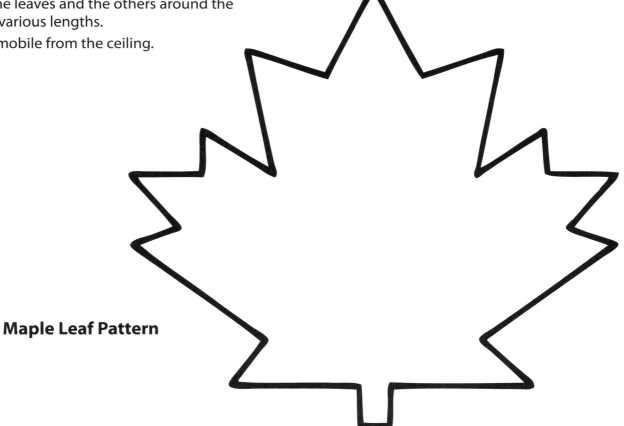

Maple Leaf Pattern

Symbols and Emblems

There are 11 Canadian provinces and two territories. Each of the provinces and territories has an identifying flag and floral emblem. All have a coat of arms with a shield that tells a story about that province or territory.

For example, the provincial coat of arms for Alberta, adopted in 1907, features the cross of St. George, symbolizing Alberta's historic association with Great Britain. Mountains and foothills stand for the Canadian Rockies. A field of wheat at the bottom represents Alberta's chief agricultural crop.

Project
Create a booklet detailing all of the provincial and territorial shields.

Materials
- Symbols and Emblems coloring pages
- construction paper or poster board
- colored pencils
- scissors
- glue
- colored construction paper
- white drawing paper

Directions
1. Using colored pencils, follow the color guides below each shield.
2. Cut around the outline of each.

3. Construct a mini-booklet out of seven pieces of white drawing paper and add a construction paper cover. Glue each shield on the top of a separate page in the booklet.
5. Research each provincial or territorial flag, coat of arms, and floral emblem. Illustrate them on the appropriate page in your booklet and include historical facts below them.

For the Teacher
Make enough copies of the Symbols and Emblems coloring pages (9–10) so that each student has 13 shields.

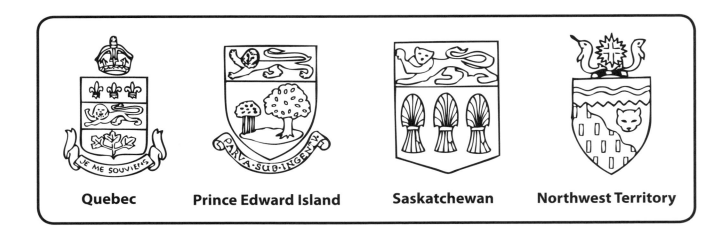

Quebec   Prince Edward Island   Saskatchewan   Northwest Territory

EP077 Canada © GHC Specialty Brands, LLC

Symbols and Emblems Coloring Page

Alberta
red cross; blue sky; white mountains; green hills;
yellow fields; white background

British Columbia
blue and red Union Jack; blue and white waves; gold sun

Manitoba
red cross on white; gold buffalo; tan
ground; green background

Nunavut
blue sky, yellow stars;
yellow ground, blue inuksuk, gray
qulliq, red flames

New Brunswick
gold lion on red; white sail; red
ship flags; brown ship on gold
background; blue water

Nova Scotia
white shield with blue cross bars;
red figure on gold background

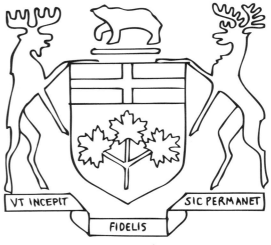

Ontario
red cross on white background;
gold maple leaves on green background

Symbols and Emblems Coloring Page

Prince Edward Island
gold lion on orange background; green trees and grass on white background

Quebec
yellow fleur-de-lis on blue; yellow lion on red; green maple leaves on yellow

Saskatchewan
red lion on gold; yellow wheat on green background

Yukon Territory
red cross on white; blue emblems on white circle; gold dots on red triangles; vertical white wavy lines on blue

Northwest Territories
wavy blue line on white; gold bars on green field; white fox on red background

Newfoundland
red shield with white cross; white animals in upper right and lower left sections, with the other two animals gold

Inuit

The Inuit are the native people of Canada's far north. Inuit meals often consisted of raw caribou meat, birds, and fish because materials for fire-building were so scarce.

Inuits lived in extreme Arctic weather conditions and used many natural resources in order to survive. Caribou antlers and hides provided the materials for harpoons, sleds, and clothing. Seal oil was used for fuel. Some Inuit lived in igloos, which were built from compact snow cut with a bone knife into blocks and stacked to form a dome. Driftwood was the only wood available. Fire was made by striking chunks of pyrite together and catching the sparks in grass. Soapstone was carved into cooking pots.

Project
Build an Inuit igloo.

Materials
- self-hardening clay
- white paint suitable for painting clay
- waxed paper
- plastic knives
- paintbrush

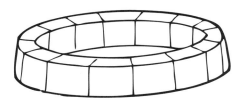

Directions
1. Form the clay into 1¼-cm (½-inch) blocks.
2. Use the plastic knife to trim the sides into flat edges.
3. On the waxed paper, form a circle with the clay blocks. Cut them to slope as shown in the illustration. Continue stacking the clay blocks, sloping inward with each row.
4. Smooth and trim the sides. When the dome shape is finished and the clay has hardened, paint the igloo white.

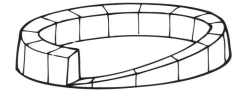

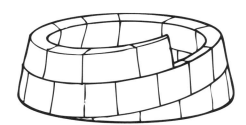

Igloo Facts
The entrance to the igloo was usually a tunnel.

Outside cracks were wedged with snow.

Inside walls were rubbed with snow, then glazed with flame.

A winter igloo usually measured 4.6 meters (15 ft) across and 3.7 meters (12 ft) high.

Native People

The first Europeans to set foot on the land that would be Canada were met by many different tribes of native people. The Micmac, Huron, Algonquin, Iroquois, and Chippewa were just a few of the tribes that extended hospitality to the settlers and fur traders.

Early visitors depended on the natives for food, shelter, and medical help. The native people of Canada lived close to and depended on nature. They taught the settlers how to use the plants and trees for shelter, canoes, baskets, and mats, and how to raise native crops such as squash and beans. Early settlers were taught to tap the maple trees for "maple water" to make syrup and sugar.

The native people traveled the many waterways of Canada in canoes, some covered in hide and some made of birch bark. Overlapping sheets of birch bark were stretched over a framework of sapling strips, then sewn over the rim of the frame. Roots of the black spruce tree were used to sew everything into place. The bark was sewn together and curved pieces of cedar were lashed to the inside. Spruce gum was used to seal the seams from water. Planks of white cedar were used to line the inside. Wood ribs were fitted over the lining, and the outside of the canoe was water-sealed.

Project
Make a canoe like the ones used by native people for transportation.

Materials
- brown poster board or construction paper
- canoe pattern
- yarn
- hole punch
- scissors

Directions
1. Trace the canoe pattern onto poster board and cut out. Use the hole punch to make holes where indicated on pattern.
2. Fold on the dotted line.
3. Using yarn, lace the ends of the canoe together.

For the Teacher
Copy one canoe pattern (page 13) per student.

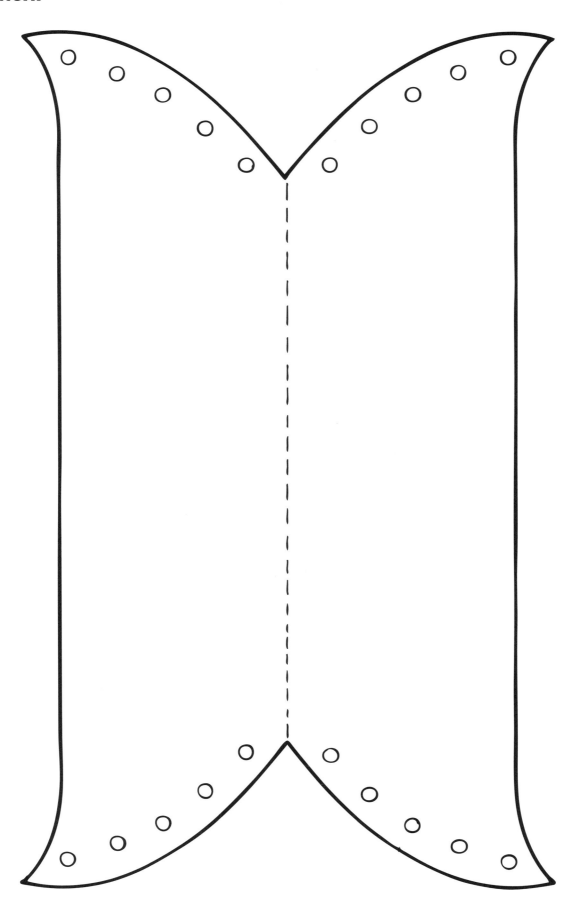

Native Resources

The native people used natural sources for housing. The Micmac built grass lodgings called wigwams, which they would cover with furs in winter. Hides and birch bark were attached to wooden frames to make teepees.

Project

Make a wigwam like the ones used by the native people for shelter.

Materials

- margarine or whipped topping container
- brown construction paper
- dried grass, raffia, or straw
- glue

Directions

1. Turn container upside down. Cut a small opening for the door.
2. Tear construction paper into small pieces and glue in an overlapping pattern onto the container.
3. Glue grass to paper-covered container, covering it completely.

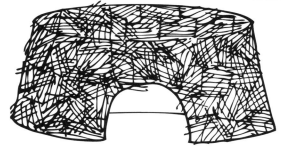

The Assiniboin depended on huge herds of bison for their food, clothing, and shelter. The Chippewa relied on caribou for the same needs. These large animals supplied meat, hide for clothing and shelter, and bone and sinew for tools and utensils. Meat was never wasted, but shared with the entire tribe. Horns were used for drinking cups. Hair from the neck was woven into rope and combined with natural objects to make ornaments.

Project

Make a bison-hair bracelet.

Materials

- brown yarn or twine
- small shells or other natural objects, drilled with a small hole
- small feathers

Directions

1. Cut several lengths of yarn, 30 cm (12 in) long. Tie together at one end.
2. Braid the strands of yarn, threading shells into the braid at intervals.
3. Weave feathers into braid.
4. Tie the ends of the yarn together, adjusting to fit around your wrist.

EP077 **Canada** © GHC Specialty Brands, LLC

Pacific Northwest Tribes

The native tribes of the Pacific Northwest lived in great wooden lodges built amidst forests of firs, cedars, and redwoods. They caught salmon, whale, and halibut for food, and wore clothing made from seal and sea otter fur. Among these tribes were the Haida, Tsimshian, Kwakiutl, Bella Coola, and Nootka. They developed great artistic skills, expressing themselves through woodworking. Examples of their work appeared in totem poles, jewelry, and elaborate masks.

It is believed that George Vancouver, a Royal Navy officer mapping the Pacific Coastline in 1788, was the first European explorer to meet these coastal inhabitants.

Project

Choose one or more crafts to complete from the Pacific Northwest Tribes Project Pages.

For the Teacher

Copy the Pacific Northwest Tribe Project Page (15–16) for each student.

Animal Deities

Animal deities were featured in many tribal crafts, dances, and ceremonies. Images were carved into the trunks of massive trees to create totem poles or statues to guard the grave of a chief. Dressed in a feather costume and beaked mask, a dancer would assume the role of a mythological bird and perform a wing-flapping ritual at the start of wedding festivities or coming-of-age ceremonies.

Materials

- variety of paper and cardboard
- feathers
- paint
- yarn
- markers
- scissors
- glue

Project

1. Use construction paper, cardboard, glue, paper plates, grocery bags, and other craft materials to create a colorful ceremonial mask to represent an imaginative animal or bird.

2. Attach yarn, if necessary, on the sides of the mask to tie it around the head.

Pacific Northwest Tribes Project Page

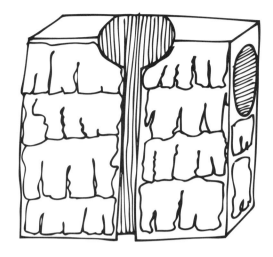

Potlatch

Important tribal events provided the occasion for a potlatch—a ceremony at which a man of high social ranking demonstrated his wealth by lavishing expensive gifts on his guests. Each recipient hosted his own potlatch at which he sought to provide gifts of greater value. A host might distribute as many as 30,000 blankets or 10,000 silver and brass bracelets or jade ornaments. These potlatches were thought to be too competitive and wasteful and the Canadian government outlawed them in 1884.

Materials
- cardboard
- paint
- sequins
- trim
- markers
- scissors
- glue

Project
Create a jeweled ornament.
1. Cut an unusual shape from cardboard.
2. Decorate the shape with bright paint, sequins, and other trims.
3. Give the ornament away during a classroom potlatch.

Cedar

Cedar was the basis of the native culture. Huge trunks provided the material for dugout canoes up to 18 meters (60 ft) long and capable of holding 50 paddlers. The gigantic tree trunks were used to frame houses 18 meters (60 ft) wide and 91 meters (300 ft) long. Narrow strips of thinly shaved bark were woven into cloaks to wear in the rain. Bright geometric designs were carved into masks, totem poles, and cedar chests in which chiefs stored their blankets.

Materials
- paper grocery bag
- brown tissue paper
- scissors
- glue

Project
Create a cedar-bark cloak.
1. Cut the center of a large brown shopping bag from bottom to top. Cut neck and arm holes.
2. Shred another shopping bag or brown tissue paper. Glue the pieces to the bag to create a shaggy appearance.

EP077 Canada

Vikings

In 1961, archaeologists discovered the ruins of a Viking settlement at L'Anse aux Meadows, on the northern tip of Newfoundland. Historians believe that the village may have been settled by Norse adventurer Leif Eriksson. The village was made up of seven turf huts, two large fire pits for roasting caribou and whale, a smithy with a stone anvil for working iron and copper, and a lumberyard. It is believed that the village housed between 100 and 140 people.

The Norse were very skilled sailors. They could sail from Norway to North America and never be more than 322 km (200 miles) from land without the use of a compass. During daylight hours, they navigated with an instrument called a *bearing dial*. At night, they navigated by observing the position of the North Star.

Project
Make a bearing dial and learn to read it.

Materials
- toilet paper tube
- 15.25 cm (6 in) paper plate
- toothpicks
- 1 egg carton section
- marker
- scissors
- glue

Directions
1. Use the marker to divide the paper plate into four equal sections. Mark directions as shown.
2. Use the toilet paper tube to trace a hole in the center of the plate and cut it out, being sure that the tube fits snugly in the hole. Slide the plate down the tube about one-quarter of the length.
3. Trim the egg carton section to fit the top of the toilet paper tube. Break a toothpick in half, inserting one piece in the top of the egg carton and one in the side of the carton as illustrated. Glue the toothpicks to secure.
4. Glue the egg carton section onto the top of the tube.

To Use: *In northern latitudes, shadows point north at noon. Align the shadow of the upright pin to the "N" mark on the dial to determine direction.*

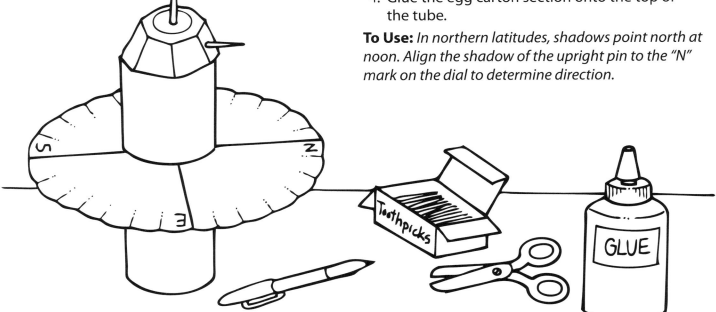

French Heritage

Nearly one quarter of the population of Canada is French Canadian, most living in the province of Quebec. The blue flag iris is the provincial flower of Quebec. The provincial flag features a *fleur-de-lis*, a stylized lily, the traditional symbol of France. The French were the first to colonize the North Atlantic Coast, called New France, during the early 1600s. It was the French who began the fur trade and who were among the first pioneers to go into the Canadian wilderness.

French Canadians of today are spread throughout Canada. However, many still have deep ties with their past and their culture, which have always been closely tied to home, family, and church. Most speak French, and many choose to follow traditional occupations like fishing and farming. Traditional celebrations, such as St. Jean Baptiste Day, and traditional foods, such as meat pies called *tourtières*, keep the French Canadian culture alive.

Project
Make an iris, or *fleur-de-lis*.

Materials
- Iris Pattern
- pencil
- bluish-purple construction paper
- green construction paper
- yellow crepe paper, cut in small shreds
- scissors
- tape
- glue

Directions
1. Trace the flower pattern onto blue construction paper and cut it out.
2. Alternating directions (up and down), curl individual petals around a pencil. Curl up-turning petals very tightly, down-turning petals more loosely.
3. Glue a few shreds of crepe paper into the center of the flower.
4. Roll the sheet of green construction paper lengthwise into a tight tube and tape closed.
5. Make several 2.54-cm (1-in) slits in one end of the tube, cutting through all layers.
6. Carefully extend the slits in the outermost layer of the paper tube to varying lengths. Fold these layers back to form leaves.
7. Fold the remaining layers outward. Glue the flower to the top of the tube.

For the Teacher
Copy one Iris pattern (page 19) per student.

EP077 *Canada* © GHC Specialty Brands, LLC

Iris Pattern

Samuel de Champlain

Samuel de Champlain was a Frenchman who explored the St. Lawrence River when he first sailed to Canada in 1603. Five years later, he chose a site on which to build a fort and trading post. It was named Quebec, the first permanent settlement in Canada.

The first winter was very cold, and even with the help of the native people, only eight of the 24 settlers survived. For 10 years, Champlain continued his explorations and his pursuit of a dream to build an empire. When he returned permanently to Quebec, he devoted himself to running the colony. With the help of Louis Hebert, known as Canada's first farmer, he created a garden where forest had been and strengthened the growth of the settlement.

Project
Plant the same crops the first settlers of Quebec planted and harvested.

Materials
- large plastic gardening containers
- corn, pea, and bean seeds
- planting soil
- gardening tools
- permanent marker
- fertilizer

Directions
1. Fill the containers with soil.
2. Plant the seeds according to the directions on the package. Label each container.
3. Tend your small gardens. Water, fertilize, and chart the growth.

Extension Activity
Imagine the difficulties the first settlers of Quebec faced when trying to grow crops in harsh winter weather. Experiment with a few of your "crops" by growing some in the classroom and some outdoors. Compare the results.

Fur Trading

Felt hats were very popular in Europe beginning in the seventeenth century. The underfur of the Canadian beaver was perfect for making felt, and the demand for the animal grew. French and British trappers led hunting expeditions into previously unexplored Canadian territory in search of these valuable animals. The fur traders fought bitter cold and disease. Meals consisted of cornmeal mush and *pemmican*, a dried meat similar to today's jerky. It was then combined with bone marrow fat (grease). Berries, when available, were added for flavoring.

The native people they befriended were given guns and traps in exchange for animal skins. They also traded for moccasins, buckskins, and canoes. Native inventions such as snowshoes and dog sleds enabled the fur traders to transport supplies and pelts when they might otherwise have failed.

Project
Play the role of a fur trader. Make a pair of snowshoes, then try to haul a heavy load of beaver pelts.

Materials
Snowshoes
- heavy yarn or twine
- cardboard
- hole punch or pencil
- marker
- scissors
- old coats

Hauling sled
- wagon or plastic sled
- rope

Directions
Showshoes

1. Stand on the cardboard and have a partner trace around the outline of each foot.

2. Measure an oval 15¼ cm (6 in) larger than each outline and cut out the cardboard.

3. Make several holes with a hole punch or sharpened pencil on opposite sides of the arch area of the outline. Lace the holes with a long piece of yarn or twine. Step on the cardboard and tie it in place over your shoe.

4. The natives' trained dogs could haul 272-kg (600-lb) loads a distance of 113 km (70 miles) a day. Pile a wagon with as many books or heavy objects as you can. Weigh each one before putting it in the wagon, then total the weight. Tie a rope to the wagon and attach it to your waist. Put on your snowshoes and pull your cargo. How much weight can you pull?

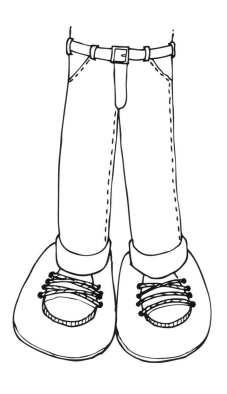

Northwest Passage

Fur traders had searched many years for the fabled Northwest Passage, a waterway on which ocean-going ships could carry their furs across the northernmost parts of the Arctic, from the Atlantic to the Pacific.

At various times, explorations were led by Jacques Cartier, Henry Hudson, and Alexander Mackenzie, among others. It was Mackenzie who became the first white man to travel over land from Canada's interior to the Pacific coast. Following maps and coastal charts filled with error and suggestion, the explorers finally decided that no such waterway existed. As a solution, the Canadian Pacific Railway, a transcontinental railroad, was built.

Project

Create a map showing a route through the northernmost Canadian territories.

Materials

- poster board
- colored pencils, marker, crayons

Directions

1. Imagine that you have heard stories about the Northwest Passage. Using the knowledge you have and stories you have heard about the Arctic, draw a map that charts the route you might take to find the passage.

2. Start by making a list of the things you might encounter—ice, bays, islands, mountains, glaciers, etc. Include them on the map.

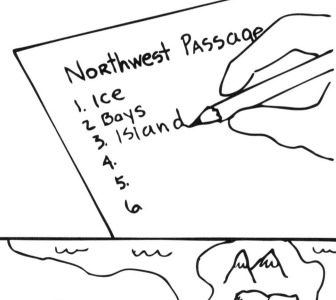

Arctic Explorers

The explorers searching for the Northwest Passage faced the harsh conditions of the Arctic. Some succeeded, others failed. The Royal Navy gave its exploring parties printed forms on which to record details of their journeys. Even though many did not survive, their stories could still be told through their journal entries.

Project

Create a journal that retells the story of an Arctic expedition in search of the Northwest Passage.

Materials

- plain writing or drawing paper
- colored pencils, markers, crayons
- stapler

Directions

1. Staple four sheets of writing paper together to form a booklet.
2. Choose an explorer below and retell their story in a picture journal.

Royal Navy Lieutenant Edward Parry—1819

Parry was the first Arctic explorer who deliberately spent a winter with his ships locked in the ice. The upper decks of his ships were roofed with quilted canvas. Heat was piped from the galley stoves. His crew existed on lime juice, vinegar, pickles, fresh bread, preserved fruits and soups, and beer brewed on ship. He sprouted seed for greens to prevent scurvy. The crew jogged on the enclosed decks and contributed articles and sketches to the expedition's newspaper.

. . . .

Royal Navy Captain John Ross—1833

Ross and his crew survived in the Arctic longer than any Europeans before them. Three winters were spent with their ship trapped in the ice. They befriended the Inuit who taught them to adapt to the environment. They learned to build sleds and snow houses. They hunted seal and bear and used the hides to make clothing. They ate animal oil and fat.

. . . .

Sir John Franklin—1847

Franklin began his expedition with 129 men, two ships, and supplies for three years. When the ships became trapped in the ice, he sent a party ahead to search for a route they could take when the ice broke up. They used dogs to pull canoes over frozen lakes. Those staying behind set out in dories to navigate through large masses of ice. They ate pemmican and corn. Not one of the men who set out with Franklin was ever seen alive again.

Hudson's Bay Company

Prince Rupert, a cousin of the King of England, and some partners founded Hudson's Bay Company in 1670. They were given a royal charter and exclusive trading rights in all the territory drained by streams that eventually flowed into the Hudson Bay. Hudson's Bay Company controlled the entire area that stretched from Hudson Bay across Canada to the Pacific, and down into what became the state of Oregon. It extended north into the Arctic regions inhabited by the Inuits.

Hides, wild rice, and native handcrafted items were exchanged for European muskets, knives, wooden barrels, tools, and liquor. Native trappers were sometimes given a brass coin which had the value of one pelt. One side bore the likeness of King George IV. The other side pictured a beaver. A hole at the top enabled it to be worn as an ornament until redeemed at the company store.

For the Teacher

Project

Reenact the trading between the native people of Canada and the Europeans of Hudson's Bay Company.

Materials

- Hudson's Bay Company Project Cards (page 25)
- materials specified for each project
- scissors
- glue

Directions

1. Divide the class into two groups: Native People and Europeans. Divide each group into four smaller groups.

2. Cut the project cards apart. Give a card (1–4) to each Native People group. Give a card (5–8) to each European group.

3. Group members follow the directions for making the project described on their card.

4. Designate an area to be the trading post. Invite the Native People to visit the Europeans in the trading post and exchange goods.

Hudson's Bay Company Project Cards

 1 Animal Pelts

The animal pelt most in demand was the beaver. Other skins that were traded were wildcat, wolverine, fox, and snowshoe hare.

Create animal pelts to trade. Cut a shape from a brown shopping bag. Fringe or crumple tissue paper in shades of brown and black. Glue the tissue paper to cover the bag.

 2 Bone and Blubber

In the east along the Labrador Coast, whalebone, oil, blubber, sealskin, and seal oil were items brought to trade.

Cut whalebone shapes from foam meat or produce trays. Make a gooey mixture of flour and water "blubber" to put into zip-top bags.

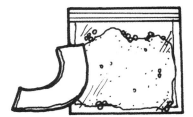

 3 Hand-Crafted Items

Items made from natural materials were traded, including sealskin boots, feather gloves, and hunting spears.

Turn paper bags into boots and old socks into gloves. Use cardboard tubes and construction paper to create spears.

 4 Coin Exchange

A brass coin, given to the Inuits by the traders, could be exchanged for goods. It was worn like a necklace or ornament until traded.

Cut 2.54-cm (1-in) circles from index cards. Paint a light shade of brown. Use a felt-tipped marker to sketch a king on one side and beaver on the other. Punch a hole at the top and string with yarn.

 5 Processed Goods

Flour, tea, sugar, and molasses were processed goods that the Europeans exchanged with the native people.

Fill clear plastic bags with the goods listed above.

 6 Metal Products

The Inuit prized metal items because they were more durable and efficient than objects made from bone and animal skins.

Use aluminum foil and cardboard to make metal tools or utensils such as spoons, nails, needles, kettles, knives, fishhooks, hammers, and axes.

 7 Manufactured Goods

Also traded were manufactured items such as woven cloth, shawls, breeches, fishnets, skeins of yarn, and glass beads.

Collect fabric remnants. Cut strips and squares of cloth for trading. Make fishing nets by tying lengths of yarn together. Wind yarn around paper tubes. Make beads from clay.

8 Iron Pots

Another popular traded item was iron pots, which were used for cooking.

Cover a large whipped topping container with foil. Punch holes on both sides for a handle. Roll a large piece of tin foil into a narrow "handle." Crinkle the ends to thread through the holes, then fold ends up to hold.

The Gold Rush

There were two major gold rushes in Canadian history. In 1858, prospectors found gold in the sandbars of the upper Fraser River, near Fort Langly. Soon after, in 1860, gold was discovered in the Cariboo Mountains in British Columbia. Miners made the difficult journey up the Fraser river to pan for gold along the shores of Quesnel and Cariboo Lakes, as well as along the many streams in the area.

The second major rush occurred in 1897. Three men discovered gold in the Klondike area of the Yukon in late 1896. Because winter was setting in and the area was extremely difficult to reach, word of the find did not leak out for months. News of the Klondike gold strike was so exciting that prospectors came from all over North America to travel the "Road of 98." Prospectors reached the area either by traveling up the Yukon River through Alaska, or by trudging over the steep Coast Mountains through the White Pass or Chilkoot Pass. Miners had to walk in single file up steep "stairs" cut in the snow, carrying a year's worth of supplies on their backs.

Panning was one of the most common ways to look for gold. A miner scooped a pan of dirt and gravel from a stream bed, stirred it to remove the lumps, then removed the rocks and pebbles. He would then wash away most of the dirt by swirling the pan of water. He placed the remainder—gold dust, nuggets, and fine sand—in the sun or by a fire. When it was dry, he blew away the sand and had his gold.

Project
Practice panning for gold.

Materials
- aluminum pie pan or iron skillet
- aquarium gravel, spray-painted gold
- mixture of sand and dirt
- dish pans or large tub
- water

Directions
1. Combine gravel, sand, dirt, and water in dish pans or tub.
2. Working outside on concrete, use the miners' method for panning for gold, spreading the remainders from the pan onto concrete to dry.

The Gold Rush

Prospectors who trudged over the Chilkoot and White Pass trails were not allowed to cross unless they carried with them enough supplies for an entire year. A mail-order catalog of the time sold a "Klondike Special" for $68.69 that included 227 kg (500 lbs) of flour, 90 kg (200 lbs) of bacon, and .45 kg (1 lb) of pepper. Many parts of the passes were too narrow and treacherous for pack animals—men would walk back and forth with their loads of supplies.

Project
Create a supply pack for a miner traveling over the Chilkoot Pass.

Materials
- paper and pencil
- food items, including flour and salt
- empty grocery bags
- pots, pans, cooking utensils
- household items and tools (see directions)
- clothing items

Directions
1. As a class, brainstorm a list of things a prospector would need to live one year in the gold fields. What kind of diet would a prospector most likely have? Include food items, household items, and tools. Don't forget the equipment needed for prospecting!
2. Gather as many of the listed items as you can. (For food items such as flour, use empty grocery bags to represent the amount needed.)
3. Divide into groups, each group devising a plan to get the supplies over the mountain. How was food preserved for packing across the mountains?

Scottish Heritage

The population of Canada reflects many different cultures. In many cases, Canadians have held on to many aspects of their ancestors' heritage—customs, foods, and music. Nearly 40 percent of modern Canadians are descended from settlers from England and Scotland who began to populate Canadian territories in the 1700s.

Across Canada, Scottish heritage is celebrated at informal gatherings called *ceilidhs* (kay-lees) and at Highland Games, which are outdoor gatherings for sporting competitions. At these events, Canadians participate in Scottish dancing and athletics. One of the most popular events is tossing a heavy wooden pole called a *caber*. Participants often dress in kilts, a skirt-like garment made of special plaid fabrics called *tartans*.

Project
Design a tartan plaid and make a Scottish kilt.

Materials
- butcher paper
- yarn
- stapler
- colored markers
- scissors

Directions
1. Measure butcher paper to fit around your waist. Cut to fit. Measure yarn to fit around your waist with enough extra to tie.

2. Choose three markers (two warm colors—red, yellow, or orange, and one cool color—blue, purple, or green).

3. Using all three colors, make a horizontal pattern of stripes, repeating the pattern to cover the paper.

4. Using two of the three colors, make a vertical pattern of stripes.

5. Lay yarn along the long edge of the butcher paper. Fold the paper over the yarn and staple in place. Wrap around your waist and tie to secure.

Mounties

The Mounties, or the Royal Canadian Mounted Police, have become as much a symbol of Canada as the beaver and the maple leaf. The Mounties were originally established in 1873 to prevent bloodshed between whiskey traders and the native people in the Northwest Territories. Riding horseback, they brought law and order to the expanding Canadian frontier.

The distinctive red coats of the Mounties were a symbol of peace; the color was chosen because the native people equated red with justice and fair dealing. The broad-brimmed hats were adopted around 1900 because they offered protection from the sun. The Mounties of today still wear the red coat for dress and ceremonial occasions, including magnificent *equestrian* demonstrations.

Project
Make a K-W-L Chart about Canadian mounties.

Materials
- poster board
- felt-tipped pen or black marker
- yard stick

Directions
1. Use a yard stick to draw lines dividing a piece of poster board into three columns.
2. At the top of the first column, neatly print K. At the top of the second column, print W. At the top of the third, print L.
3. Under the column headed "K," neatly print what you knew about Canada's mounties before you started this lesson.
4. Under the column labeled "W," print what you want or expect to learn from your research.
5. Read more about Canada's mounted police in an encyclopedia, some other book, or on the Internet. Search under "Royal Canadian Mounted Police."
6. Under the column headed "L," print important facts you learned about the mounties from your reading.

Animals

Mountains and wastelands make up more than half the land area of Canada, and forests cover about one third. Although this vast land is home to hundreds of different kinds of wildlife, some have become endangered due to over-hunting and the destruction of their ecosystem.

The Canadian government has set aside large land areas to create national parks where wildlife and their habitats are protected. Laws restricting hunting and trapping have saved some species, such as sea otters, from extinction.

Project
Choose an animal project to complete.

Materials
- Animal Project Page
- scissors
  paint and paintbrushes
- construction paper
- fabric, twigs, cotton, and other craft materials
- clay
- shoe box
- brown felt
- paint sponge
- scissors

For the Teacher
Copy one Animal Project Page (31) per student.

Animal Diorama

Directions
1. Use paint, construction paper, clay, and other craft materials to create a shoe box diorama featuring a Canadian animal in its habitat. See the suggestions below. Look through resource books to find facts and pictures to make the diorama more accurate.
   - Huge polar bears roam the icy north.
   - Beaver, otter, mink, muskrat, chipmunks, and wildcats live in the forests.
   - Caribou, moose, and elk roam freely in the wilderness. Deer are a common sight as well.
   - Moose, bighorn sheep, black bears, grizzly bears, and mountain goats are among the animals that live in the Rockies.
   - High forests are home to porcupines, chipmunks, and mountain lions.
   - Temperate rain forests abound with species such as the cougar, bald eagle, and marmot.
   - Many types of birds, including sparrows, robins, sea gulls, owls, and quail, make their nests in marshy swamps or forests.
   - Lakes are filled with herring, perch, and whitefish. The oceans are filled with cod, scallops, salmon, and lobster.

Animal Project Page

Canada Goose

The Canada goose measures 41 to 64 cm (16 to 25 in) in length and has a grayish-brown coat with white patches on its cheeks. Its head, neck, and tail are primarily black. It uses twigs, weeds, grass, and reeds to make its nest on a mound in a marsh. It lines its nest with downy feathers. The nest holds from five to nine pale green, yellowish, or buff-white eggs. In the autumn, their distinctive honking can be heard as the families migrate south for the winter months, flying in a perfect V-formation.

Directions

1. Use tempera paint to sponge paint a landscape background of a marsh or sky.

2. When the background paint has dried, cut and glue construction paper to depict a family of geese flying south in a V-formation. Add dimension by gluing cotton in the sky.

Beaver

The beaver, a Canadian national symbol, is found in rivers, streams, and fresh-water lakes near woodlands. An excellent swimmer, a beaver can stay underwater for .8 km (.5 miles) and can hold its breath for up to 15 minutes. A beaver uses its tail to steer when it swims, as a prop when it stands on its hind legs, and as a warning signal by slapping it on the water to create a loud noise. The beaver's teeth are sharp and hard and are used for cutting down small trees. Beaver fur is soft and shiny. Its color varies from dark brown to yellowish brown. When beaver fur is squeezed together with other kinds of fur to make a cloth, it is called *felt*.

Directions

1. Paint a scene on white construction paper showing a beaver in action. The beaver might be swimming underwater, building a dam or lodge, cutting down a tree, or slapping its tail on the water. Include the background in your painting.

2. Cut a felt tail for the beaver and glue it in place in the painting.

Forestry

Almost half of Canada's land is covered with forest. The forests are made up of many kinds of trees, including cedar, hemlock, fir, and pine. These trees were used for many of the needs of the native people: materials for homes and canoes; leaves, bark, and mosses for medicines; and shelter and food for the animals they hunted.

The lumber industry grew along with the fur trade as early settlers made their way across the Canadian frontier. Present-day Canada is still one of the leading lumber-producing nations of the world. The numerous lakes and rivers provide a natural transportation system for logs and other products of the industry. Christmas tree farms in Nova Scotia, Quebec, and New Brunswick send trees as far away as South America.

Project

Make a guidebook of Canadian trees.

Materials

- construction paper
- markers or colored pencils

Directions

1. Pick a number of species and devote one page of your book to each tree. Draw a picture of each tree's leaf/needle shape and color.

2. Draw a picture of the bark and profile of the tree.

3. Write a paragraph about each tree (its uses, territory, elevation, etc.)

4. Make a cover for your book. Glue tissue paper leaves to trunks you have drawn with a crayon or marker.

5. Bind your book by stapling the cover and pages together.

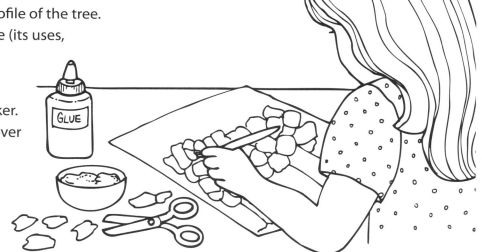

Extension Activity

Brainstorm a list of products that are part of the forestry industry—for example, paper and pulpwood. Look around the classroom and in your home for ideas.

Lumber

The site of a log cabin sitting in a clearing is still very common in Canada, a reminder of the past. Lumber from Canada's sawmills is shipped all over the country, as well as to their neighbor to the south, the United States, and faraway places, like Japan.

Canadians proudly celebrate the heritage of their pioneer background. Festivals such as Klondike Days in Edmonton, Alberta, give Canadians an opportunity to test their skills as lumberjacks. Similar celebrations are held all across Canada. Contests might include sawing competitions and ox-pulls, in which oxen must pull heavy weights. In a log-rolling contest, two people balance on a log floating in water, each attempting to get the other dumped into the water!

For the Teacher

Project
Play a "lumberjack" relay game.

Materials
- plaid long-sleeved shirt and knit cap for each team
- wooden boards, one per team
- butcher paper
- markers or crayons

Directions
1. Divide into two or more teams.
2. Place the boards next to each other, several meters from the two teams. Place butcher paper either on an easel or a wall, on the opposite end of the boards from the teams' starting place.
3. The first runner on each team must put on the lumberjack's shirt and cap, then run to the board and walk across it. Be careful to keep your balance!
4. Once across, the runner goes to the butcher paper and draws a tree. (Good lumberjacks reforest the areas where they've been cutting!) The runner then recrosses the board, returns to his or her team, and passes the shirt and cap on to the next person. The first team to have all their lumberjacks back from the forest wins!

Banff National Park

The area that would become Banff National Park was found in 1883 when three Canadian Pacific Railway workers found a cave with hot springs in the eastern portion of Alberta's Rocky Mountains. In 1887 it became Canada's first national park and the third national park in the world. Banff is known around the world as a park with majestic scenery and wildlife—there are nearly 1,000 different types of flowers, trees, and grasses, and about 56 species of mammals!

Banff National Park is 6,641 sq. km. (2,564 sq. mi.) and today is a popular site for camping, hiking, and many other outdoor activities.

Project
Make a classroom mural of Banff National Park.

Materials
- research materials
- large piece of butcher paper
- pencils, markers, crayons
- art and craft supplies

Directions
1. Divide into teams and research either the landscape, plants, or animals of Banff National Park. Use encyclopedias, pictures, and the Internet.

2. On a large piece of butcher paper, the landscape team should draw the landscape of Banff. Be sure to include mountains in the background!

3. Once the landscape team is finished, the plant team should add their drawings or use craft materials to make three-dimensional plant life.

4. After the plants are drawn in, the animals should be added.

For the Teacher
Divide students into teams and assign each team a group to research and draw. Help students identify and draw landscapes, plants, and animals typical of Banff National Park on the mural. When the mural is done, post it on a wall in the classroom!

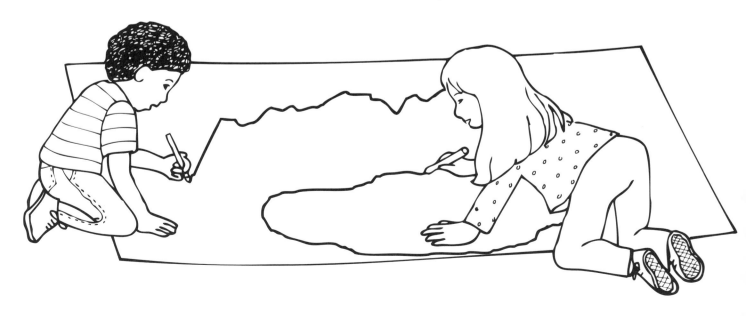

Bay of Fundy

The world's highest tides occur in Canada at The Bay of Fundy. The Bay of Fundy is located between New Brunswick and Nova Scotia. About 380 billion liters (100 billion gallons) of water flow in and out of the bay daily. The tides are caused by the gravitational pull by the moon that affects all of the waters on earth. This pull, combined with the shape of the bay, creates the perfect area for 15 meter (50-foot) tides.

The Fundy Bay area is surrounded by sandstone cliffs, plateaus, and many strange rock formations, all of which have been carved out by erosion. Fundy Bay is home to eight species of whale, about 248 species of birds, and many other animals including dolphins, fish, seals, and more!

Project
Create a travel brochure for The Bay of Fundy.

Materials
- research materials
- paper
- pencil, crayons, markers

Directions
1. Research more about the Bay of Fundy. Learn about what can be done there, what a visitor can expect to see, etc.
2. Fold a piece of paper into three sections. Make the front section a cover page. Come up with an exciting slogan and an eye-catching drawing!
3. Fill the inside of the brochure with statistical information, activities, and more.
4. On the back cover, be sure to include your "travel agency" name!

Sports

The people of Canada are enthusiastic about sports for all seasons. Hockey and other ice sports, as well as baseball and lacrosse, are an important part of Canadian life.

Some sports, like curling, were imported from other nations, but others were developed in Canada. Lacrosse evolved from baggataway, a game played by the Algonquins of the St. Lawrence River Valley as a way of training warriors for battle. Ice hockey, Canada's national sport, was introduced in Canada in the early 1800s. The first recorded use of a puck instead of a ball occurred in 1860. By the 1880s, several amateur clubs and leagues were organized in Canada. The rules for another world-popular sport, basketball, were drawn up in 1891 by James Naismith, a Canadian-born physician who was interested in sports.

For the Teacher

Project
Plan a Sports Day to learn and demonstrate Canadian sports.

Materials
- rule books and sports equipment for suggested games, page 37

Directions
1. Select which games will be demonstrated and gather necessary equipment.
2. Divide class into groups. Each group will be responsible for mastering the skills and safety regulations for one game.
3. Create a schedule that allows students to rotate through the game areas, learning and playing as they go along.

Alternate Activity
For younger students, or if you do not have time to play the sports listed, consider bringing in recorded sporting events for students to watch.

Canadian Sports

Hockey

Those who first played this game used a lacrosse ball and field-hockey sticks. Later, players used a wooden disk or cow's kneecap as a puck. Originally it was played with as many players as wanted to participate, and the game was over when a team made three goals or if a player fell through the ice.

A hockey team is made up of six players. Players score points by hitting a round disk, called a puck, into the goal cage or net. Hockey is exciting and fast-paced. It has become very popular in many countries, especially Russia, Czechoslovakia, Sweden, and the United States.

Lacrosse

Lacrosse was developed in Canada and has become popular throughout Australia, England, and the United States. The game originated with the native people of Canada, and often involved thousands of players.

The object of lacrosse is to score a goal by throwing, scooping, or kicking a rubber ball into the opposing teams' goal. The ball is moved with a stick that has a net pocket at one end. It is the stick that gives lacrosse its name— *la crosse*, French for *the stick*. The ball used is slightly smaller than a baseball, and can travel up to 160 km (100 miles) per hour.

Ringette

Ringette is very similar to ice hockey and is usually played by girls and women. It was invented in Ontario, Canada, and is now played in the northern United States as well as some European countries.

Teams of six skaters try to score goals by pushing a hollow rubber ring into a net on either end of the ice rink. Ringette sticks are straight, not curved like hockey sticks. No body contact is allowed. As in hockey, protective equipment such as knee and elbow pads and helmets with face masks are worn.

Curling

Another ice sport, curling, was brought to Canada from Scotland in 1759. Curling was developed in Scotland and the Netherlands around 400 years ago. Four-skater teams slide granite stones down an ice rink, aiming toward a 3.7-m (12-ft) target or *house*.

The 6.6-kg (14½-lb) stone is flung first by its handle. The ice in front of the stone is "swept" with a "broom" by team members to decrease any resistance for the stone during its movement into the house. When the stone is flung, it "curls," giving the game its name. Points are scored for the stones landing closest to the center of the house.

Canada Day

Canadians celebrated their country's first birthday on July 1, 1868, when the provinces of Ontario, Quebec, Nova Scotia, and New Brunswick united to form one country. The other provinces and territories joined later. The official holiday, originally known as Dominion Day, was established in 1879. In 1982, the name was changed to Canada Day. Giant birthday parties take place throughout the country. Some communities share a large birthday cake. Others put on fireworks displays. Choirs sing, bands play, and dancers perform.

Project

Research and celebrate Canada Day with a variety of activities.

- How do other countries' National Holidays (such as the fourth of July in the United States) compare to Canada Day? What are they celebrating—the joining of territories, the ending of a war, freedom from another country? What kinds of events and customs do countries share when celebrating? What kinds of things are different? Make two lists, one for similar things and one for different things.

- Make a time line of Canada's becoming a nation. Include when provinces first became provinces, then when they each joined to become Canada.

- Plan a parade with floats and patriotic music. Dress in costumes that reflect the history of Canada. Your parade should include explorers, trappers, soldiers, and Mounties. Invite other classes to come and watch.

Canada Day Newspaper

Project

Pretend you are a reporter for The Calgary Sun, a daily Canadian newspaper. Write the lead paragraph to a news story you will write describing one of the activities that took place during Canada Day celebrations in your city on July 1. Be sure to include in your paragraph answers to the five "W" questions (Who? What? When? Where? and Why?) that make up a good lead paragraph. Also, remember to print the name of your newspaper at the top, along with the date and a headline for your story.

Include a lead paragraph for a feature, or human interest story on how your fellow classmates celebrate Canada Day. Write a paragraph and make a graph with the info from your interviews. How many classmates attend fireworks displays, how many have a picnic, how many see a parade, etc.

Materials

- white construction paper
- pencil or pen
- front page of a sample newspaper to use as a guide

Directions

1. Print the name of the newspaper at the top of your paper in large letters.
2. Write the date below the name of the newspaper.
3. Print the headline to your story in letters slightly smaller than those used to write the name of your newspaper.
4. Write your lead paragraph to your news story. Below that include your feature story lead paragraph and graph.

Note: *Additional information about Canada Day can easily be found on the Internet.*

Canada Day Bookmark

Project

Make a bookmark honoring Sir John A. Macdonald, the first prime minister of Canada.

Materials

- poster board, card stock, or the top or bottom of a white gift box
- pen or pencil; colored pencils or crayons
- scissors and hole punch
- clear contact paper
- ribbon
- research materials

Directions

1. Cut a bookmark measuring 5 x 15 cm (2 x 6 in) from poster board, card stock, or a gift box.
2. Color the picture of Sir John A. Macdonald below. Cut out around it and attach to your bookmark. Write his name under the drawing.
3. On the back, neatly print a few sentences about why Sir Macdonald is referred to as the "father of present-day Canada. " Again, consult an encyclopedia or the Internet.
4. Use either colored pencils or crayons to make both sides of your bookmark eye-appealing.
5. Cover both sides with clear contact paper. Punch a hole in the top and insert a colorful ribbon.

Victoria Day

May 24 marks the birthday of Queen Victoria, the British sovereign who was queen when Canada was established by Great Britain in 1867. Since that event, her birthday has been celebrated in various ways. At one rural post, Mounties staged a snake-killing competition! Victorians of the late nineteenth century held a regatta of small craft. Victoria Day officially became a holiday in 1952, and is celebrated either on May 24 or on the Monday preceding it. Today it is traditionally celebrated with great displays of fireworks. On the same day, people in Quebec celebrate *Fete de Dollard des Ormeaux*, honoring a soldier killed during colonial times.

Queen Victoria never visited Canada, yet her influence is still evident. It was Queen Victoria who chose Ottawa as the capital of the United Province of Canada. The province of Alberta was named for her daughter, Princess Louise Caroline Alberta.

Project

Make a crown in honor of the British monarch Queen Victoria. Research facts and write questions about Queen Victoria.

Materials

- crown pattern
- tape
- paintbrush
- scissors
- pencil
- drawing paper

Directions

1. Cut out the crown and jewel patterns. Color the crown yellow or gold.
2. Tape the two crowns together to form a circle.
3. Write a question about Queen Victoria on each jewel front. Write the answers to your questions on the back of each jewel. Match the dot on each jewel to the dot on each crown point. Staple or glue just at that point.
4. See if your classmates can answer all the questions on your crown.

For the Teacher

Copy two crown patterns (page 41) per student.

Extension Activity

Hold a contest in which teams try to locate city and provincial names and other Canadian heritage locales and events which are named for Queen Victoria or a member of her family.

EP077 Canada © GHC Specialty Brands, LLC

Crown Pattern

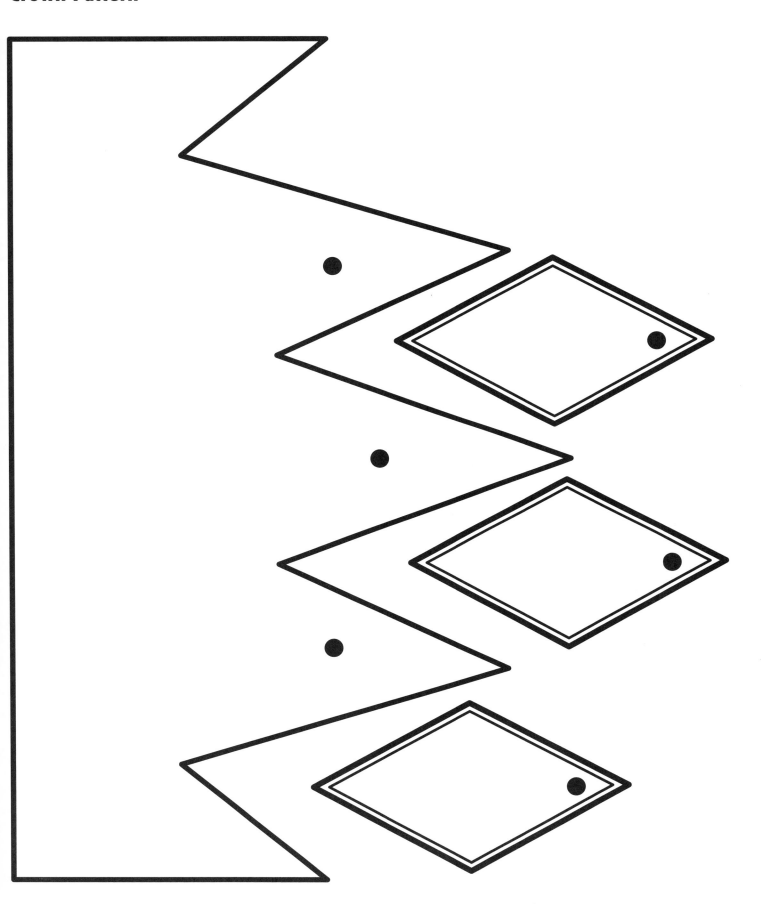

Quebec Winter Carnival

Long, harsh winters are a part of Canadian life. Newcomers to this cold land learned to brighten the cold months with winter sports and recreation. By the nineteenth century, Canadians, especially those in Quebec, were making winter fun with skating, sleighing, snowshoeing, snowball battles, and outdoor dances, concerts, and picnics.

North America's first winter carnival was staged in Montreal, Quebec, in 1894. Hundreds of people participated in five days of curling, sleigh-rides, tobogganing, snowshoeing, hockey, and fireworks. Later festivals featured elaborate ice palaces, carved from huge chunks of ice.

Project

Throw a winter festival for your class!

Materials

- poster board—one white, one blue, and assorted other colors
- large cardboard boxes
- crayons, markers, colored pencils
- construction paper, assorted colors
- scissors, masking tape
- small round magnets and one bar magnet

For the Teacher

Break the class up into three groups and assign each group one of the activities to complete. Once all groups are finished, have each group discuss their part of the project, post the mascot on the board, then let students tour the palace and play the games!

Mascot

The mascot of the Quebec Winter Carnival is a snowman named Bonhomme Carnaval. If you had to choose a mascot for your classroom's winter carnival, what would it be? Think of what the mascot would look like and wear, what it would symbolize, and what its name would be. On a large piece of white poster board, draw a sketch of your festival's mascot.

Ice Palace

One of the most elaborate parts of the Quebec Winter Carnival is the ice palace. Create an ice palace for your classroom's winter festival. Using cardboard boxes, poster board, and other materials, create an ice palace that your classmates can walk through. Don't forget to decorate it, inside and out!

Games

At the Quebec Winter Carnival, there are many games and sports played. Set up some winter games to be played at your station.
Target practice—Cut a six-inch-diameter hole in a piece of cardboard. Wad up pieces of paper or use foam balls, and try to throw them through the hole. Put a piece of tape on the floor to tell players where to stand while throwing.
Ice fishing—Cut fish shapes from pieces of construction paper. Glue a small round magnet to each fish, and place the fish magnet-up on a piece of blue poster board. Tie fishing line to a long dowel, and tie a bar magnet to the other end of the fishing line. Players may not step on poster board while fishing!
Snow Sculptures—Create snow sculptures out of snow or carved foam. Have a contest to see whose sculpture is judged Most Creative, Prettiest, etc.

Calgary Stampede

For 10 days during every summer, the citizens of Calgary, Alberta, don western clothes and cowboy hats to celebrate the mythology of the old frontier with the Calgary Stampede. Calgary was built on the frontier economy of cattle, wheat, oil, and natural gas. This yearly rodeo event celebrates the city's history.

The entire town is redecorated to look like an old western town, and it is not unusual to find horses in the street and tethered to parking meters. The streets are filled with music coming from loudspeakers. People come from all over the world to watch bucking broncos, steer-wrestling, wild-horse races, and chuck-wagon races.

For the Teacher
Stage a chuck-wagon race.

Materials
- wagon for each team
- empty food containers, such as boxes and aluminum cans
- construction cones, boxes, or other items to use as barriers

Directions
1. Arrange cones, boxes, and barriers to make an obstacle course.
2. Divide the class into equal teams.
3. Each relay team runs the obstacle course, pulling a wagon filled with identical loads of food containers. If anything spills from the wagon, the runner must stop and reload.

Regional Food

The many cultures that have contributed to the growth of Canada have also added to the variety of foods enjoyed by the people who live there. The early inhabitants of Canada ate off the land, adapting native plants and animals to their use. Inuits ate muktuk (whale skin and blubber).

Today, each region of the country has its specialties—British Columbia and the Maritime Provinces are known for seafood; the Prairies are known for their excellent beef; Quebec has developed a French Canadian cuisine; and in the Northwest Territories, moose meat and fresh lake fish are popular.

Project
Plan a feast and sample foods that are popular in Canada.

Materials
- white paper tablecloth
- red tempera paint and paint brush
- maple leaf pattern (page 7)
- poster board
- scissors
- see individual recipes for ingredients

Directions
1. Use the maple leaf pattern (page 7) and scissors to make a stencil from poster board.
2. With tempera paint and a brush, stencil a maple leaf pattern to decorate the tablecloth or make signs identifying each dish.
3. Break into groups for preparation of the recipes. See individual recipes for directions.

Habitant Pea Soup

This is a French Canadian dish adapted from the traditional food carried by voyageurs on their long trips.

Ingredients
- 550 g (1¼ lbs) dried green peas
- 225 g (½ lb) salt pork
- 2½ L (10½ cups) water
- 60 ml (¼ cup) chopped parsley
- 120 ml (½ cup) chopped celery
- 3 bay leaves
- 5 ml (1 tsp.) pepper
- 5 ml (1 tsp.) savory
- 2 diced onions

Directions
1. Wash and drain peas and put them in a soup pot with water. Boil for 2 minutes; remove from heat and cool for two hours.
2. Add remaining ingredients. Bring soup to a boil again, then turn down heat and simmer 2 hours.

Recipes

Tourtiere

Tourtiere is a pork pie that is a traditional favorite in the province of Quebec.

Ingredients

- 907 g (2 lbs) ground pork
- 1 clove garlic, crushed
- 1 medium onion, chopped
- 120 ml (½ cup) water
- salt
- 1¼ ml (¼ tsp.) celery salt
- 1¼ ml (¼ tsp.) ground cloves
- pastry for double-crust pie shell
- 60 ml (¼ cup) dry bread crumbs
- pepper

Directions

1. Combine all ingredients except bread crumbs and pastry shell in saucepan.
2. Add salt and pepper to taste.
3. Simmer until meat and onions are tender, about 20 minutes. Stir in bread crumbs and let cool.
4. Line pie pan with half of pastry and cover with pork filling. Cover with other half of pastry and cut vent holes.
5. Bake at 175˚ C (350˚ F) until browned, about 35 minutes. Let sit several minutes before serving.

Bannock

This bread was first made by the native people, who baked it over an open fire. European settlers fried it in a pan.

Ingredients

- 480 ml (2 cups) flour
- 480 ml (2 cups) water
- pinch salt
- 15 ml (1 Tbsp.) baking powder
- 1 egg
- 15 ml (1 Tbsp.) sugar
- vegetable oil
- jam

Directions

1. Mix flour, water, salt, and baking powder in a large bowl. Add egg and sugar, mixing well.
2. Heat a small amount of oil in a frying pan. Pour one-third of batter into a pan and cook until small bubbles appear. Add more oil and flip the bannock over. Cook until second side is done.
3. Repeat with remaining batter.
4. Cut bannocks into pieces and serve with jam.

Recipes

Maple Syrup Shortbreads

It takes 151 L (40 gallons) of maple sap to make 4.5 L (1 gallon) of pure maple syrup.

Ingredients

- 120 ml (½ cup) butter
- 60 ml (¼ cup) sugar
- 240 ml (1 cup) flour
- 180 ml (¾ cup) brown sugar
- 120 ml (½ cup) maple syrup
- 15 ml (1 Tbsp.) butter, at room temperature
- 1 egg, at room temperature
- 5 ml (1 tsp.) vanilla
- 120 ml (½ cup) chopped nuts

Directions

1. Cream butter with sugar in a large mixing bowl, using a spoon or electric mixer. Add flour, a little at a time, mixing continually, and blend well. Do not form into ball.

2. Pat mixture into the bottom of greased 20-cm (8-in) baking pan. Bake at 175° C (350° F) about 25 minutes, or until light brown.

3. In a medium bowl, blend brown sugar, maple syrup, and 15 ml (1 Tbsp.) butter. Add egg and vanilla and mix until smooth. Pour evenly over shortbread and sprinkle with nuts. Return to oven and bake until topping sets, about 20 minutes. Cool completely and cut into 3.8 cm (1½ in) squares.

Canadian Apple Cake

Apples and maple syrup are two of Canada's most plentiful products.

Ingredients

- 360 ml (1½ cups) sifted flour
- 120 ml (½ cup) sugar
- 5 ml (1 tsp.) baking powder
- 2.5 ml (½ tsp.) salt
- 120 ml (½ cup) shortening
- 120 ml (½ cup) milk
- 1 egg, beaten
- 3 apples, peeled, cored, and finely sliced
- 10 ml (2 tsp.) ground cinnamon
- 30 ml (2 Tbsp.) butter
- 30 ml (2 Tbsp.) maple syrup

Directions

1. Sift flour, 45 ml (3 Tbsp.) of the sugar, baking powder, and salt in mixing bowl. Cut in shortening with two knives or a pastry blender. Stir in milk and eggs to form a soft dough.

2. Spread dough smoothly in a 20-cm (8-in) square baking pan and lay overlapping slices of apple in rows on the dough. Mix remaining sugar and cinnamon and sprinkle over apples. Dot with butter. Bake at 190° C (375° F) for about 50 minutes or until toothpick comes out clean when inserted in cake. Remove from oven and drizzle maple syrup over the top.

Literature List

Check with your librarian for other recommended titles on Canada and its people.

The Broken Blade
by William Durbin. Yearling, 1998. 176 pp. Gr. 4–6.
When Pierre LaPage's father has an accident, the 13-year-old quits school and paddles a canoe 2400 miles as a voyageur for the North West Company in order to earn money for his family.

Call of the Wild
by Jack London. Scholastic Paperbacks, 2001. 192 pp. Gr. 4–6.
Stolen from his family, a dog named Buck must quickly learn the harsh law of survival among the men and dogs of the Klondike Gold Fields.

Canada ABCs: A Book about the People and Places of Canada
by Brenda Haugen. Picture Window Books, 2004. 32 pp. Gr. 2–5.
An alphabetical exploration of the people, geography, animals, plants, history, and culture of Canada.

Canada: The People
by Bobbie Kalman. Crabtree Press, 2002. 32 pp. Gr. 4–6.
Examines various aspects of life in Canada, including school, work, play, the French and British heritage, immigration, and issues that must be resolved with native peoples and the French-speaking population in Quebec.

Crazy about Canada: Amazing Things Kids Want to Know.
by Vivien Bowers. Maple Tree Press, 2007. 96 pp. Gr. 1–3.
Questions and answers from Canadian kids about all kinds of things Canadian in a colorful and fun format.

First Peoples: The Inuit of Canada
by Danielle Corriveau. Lerner Publications, 2002. 48 pp. Gr. 4–6.
Introduction to the history and culture of the Inuit.

The Gift of the Inuksuk
by Michael Ulmer. Sleeping Bear Press, 2004. 32 pp. Gr. 2–3.
In this original Pourquoi story, a young girl builds stone men, called Inuksuk, to guide her father and brother home when they are lost in a storm while hunting caribou.

The Lamp, the Ice, and the Boat Called Fish: Based on a True Story
by Jacqueline Briggs T. Martin, Houghton Mifflin, 2001. 48 pp. Gr. 2–4.
Tells the dramatic story of the Canadian Arctic Expedition that set off in 1913 to explore the high north.

Mystery at Chilkoot Pass
by Barbara A. Steiner. (American Girl History Mysteries). Pleasant Company Publications, 2001. 160 pp. Gr. 3–6.
At the start of the Klondike gold rush of 1897, while traveling through Canada with her father, uncle and friends, 12-year-old Hetty tries to determine the identity of a thief.

North
by Donna Jo Napoli. Greenwillow, 2004. 352 pp. Gr. 4–6.
Tired of his mother's over-protectiveness and intrigued by the life of African American explorer Matthew Henson, 12-year-old Alvin travels north and spends a season with a trapper near the Arctic Circle.

The Red Sash
by Jean E. Pendziwol. Groundwood Books, 2005. 40 pp. Gr. 1–3.
This short fiction story tells the story of the Canadian fur trade in the early years of the nineteenth century through the eyes of a Métis boy.

Emblems of the Territories and Provinces
http://www.saskschools.ca/~gregory/canada/emblems.html

Maple Syrup Information
http://www.canadianmaplesyrup.com/maplehistory.html

Glossary

Acadians—French settlers in the area now known as Nova Scotia

bearing dial—a navigational instrument used during daylight hours by Vikings

caber—a heavy wooden pole used by the Scottish for tossing games

Canadian Pacific Railway—a transcontinental railroad

ceilidh—an informal celebration featuring Scottish music, dance, and storytelling

deity—a god

dories—small, flat-bottomed, high-sided boats with sharp prows

equestrian—having to do with horse riding

fleur-de-lis—the ancient French symbol that appears on the flag of Quebec. The name means "flower of the lily," and its shape resembles an iris

habitant—the rural farmers of New France

igloo—a shelter built by the Inuit, made of blocks of snow

Inuit—Eskimo people of Arctic Canada

inuksuk—stone monuments that guide the people on the land and mark sacred and other special places

kilt—traditional Scottish skirt-like garment

L'Anse aux Meadows—a site on the northernmost tip of Newfoundland where archeologists discovered the ruins of a Viking settlement

lumberjack—a person whose work is to cut down timber and prepare it for the sawmill

Micmac—native people of eastern Canada. First encountered by Cartier in his explorations, they helped the European settlers adapt to life in New France

Mounties—shortened term for Royal Canadian Mounted Police

New France—the name given to Canada by the first European explorers

Northwest Passage—the legendary water route across the North American continent that many explorers hoped to find

Parliament—Canada's governing body

pemmican—food substance made of dried meat and berries, kneaded together with fat, and shaped into patties. It could be stored for long periods of time and was easy to take on long expeditions.

potlatch—celebration at which a host of the native people displays his wealth and social standing by giving away food and lavish gifts

Queen Victoria—reigning queen during the establishment of Canada in 1867

qulliq—an Inuit stone lamp

tartan—a plaid pattern with stripes of different widths and colors, originally worn by the Scots in Scotland. Each clan, or group of families, has its own pattern

totem—animal or natural object taken as a symbol for a family or clan

voyageur—French term for the adventurers who explored unknown areas of Canada in search of animal pelts for trading

wigwam—a type of tent used by some tribes of native people; shaped in a dome or cone and covered with bark, grass, woven mats, leaves, or other natural materials

EP077 *Canada* © GHC Specialty Brands, LLC